APR   2017

Westminster Public Library
3705 W. 112th Avenue
Westminster, CO 80031
www.westminsterlibrary.org

Holidays

Memorial Day

by R.J. Bailey

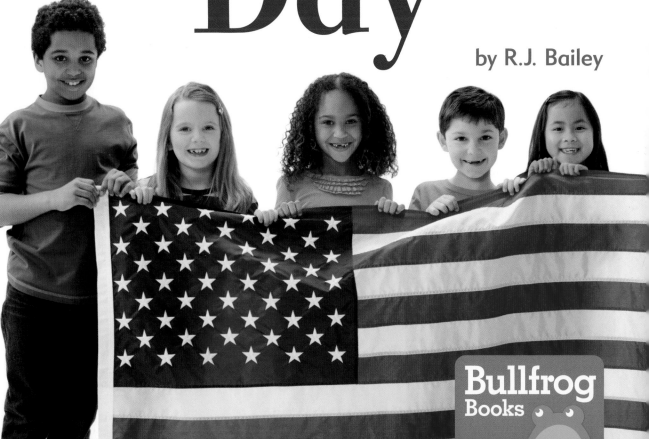

Bullfrog Books

Ideas for Parents and Teachers

Bullfrog Books let children practice reading informational text at the earliest reading levels. Repetition, familiar words, and photo labels support early readers.

Before Reading

- Discuss the cover photo. What does it tell them?

- Look at the picture glossary together. Read and discuss the words.

Read the Book

- "Walk" through the book and look at the photos. Let the child ask questions. Point out the photo labels.

- Read the book to the child, or have him or her read independently.

After Reading

- Prompt the child to think more. Ask: How do you celebrate Memorial Day? What sorts of things do you see when it's Memorial Day?

Bullfrog Books are published by Jump!
5357 Penn Avenue South
Minneapolis, MN 55419
www.jumplibrary.com

Copyright © 2017 Jump! International copyright reserved in all countries. No part of this book may be reproduced in any form without written permission from the publisher.

Library of Congress Cataloging-in-Publication Data

Names: Bailey, R.J. author.
Title: Memorial Day / by R.J. Bailey.
Description: Minneapolis, Minnesota: Jump!, Inc. [2017] | Series: Holidays | Includes index.
Audience: Grades K-3.
Identifiers: LCCN 2016007140 (print)
LCCN 2016008022 (ebook)
ISBN 9781620313558 (hard cover: alk. paper)
ISBN 9781624964022 (e-book)
Subjects: LCSH: Memorial Day—Juvenile literature.
Classification: LCC E642 .B17 2017 (print)
LCC E642 (ebook) | DDC 394.262—dc23
LC record available at http://lccn.loc.gov/2016007140

Editor: Kirsten Chang
Series Designer: Ellen Huber
Book Designer: Michelle Sonnek
Photo Researchers: Kirsten Chang & Michelle Sonnek

Photo Credits: All photos by Shutterstock except: Adobe Stock, 6–7, 8, 22tl; Age Fotostock, 20–21; Alamy, 15; Bryan Busovicki/Shutterstock.com, 22br; Corbis, 10–11; Joe Ravi/Shutterstock.com, 3; Superstock, 1, 14; Thinkstock, 12–13, 14, 16–17, 18–19, 24; Tupungato/Shutterstock.com, 23tl.

Printed in the United States of America at Corporate Graphics in North Mankato, Minnesota.

Table of Contents

What Is Memorial Day?

Memorial Day is in May.

It is on the last Monday.

What do we do on this day?

We remember
soldiers who
died in war.

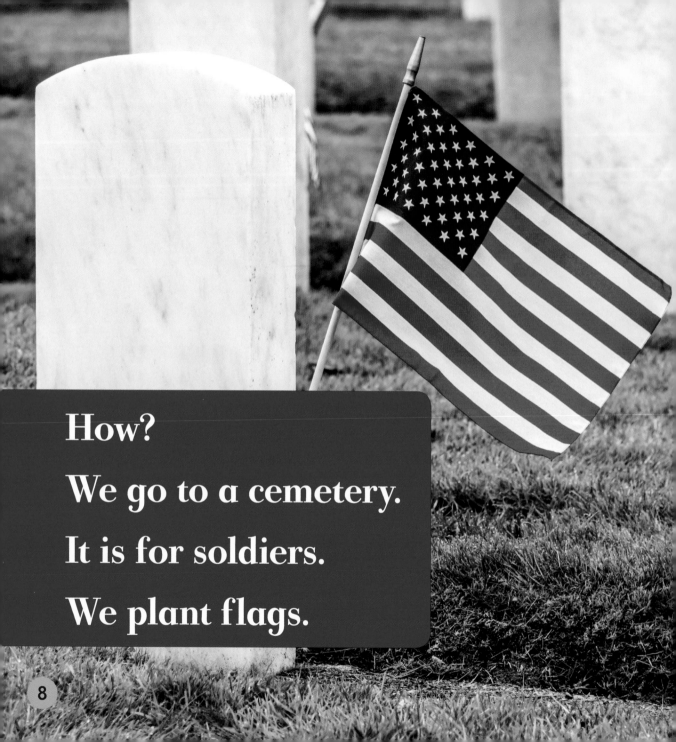

How?

We go to a cemetery.

It is for soldiers.

We plant flags.

We bring a wreath.

Meg visits a
war memorial.

We wear a paper flower.

It is a poppy.

poppy

We watch a concert.

It is on TV.

Look! It's a singer!

We eat outside.
Mom makes hot dogs.
Yum!

We close our eyes.

We hold hands.

We think of the soldiers who died for our country.

19

Thank you for
your service!

We honor
your memory.

Symbols of Memorial Day

flag

flowers

soldier

war monument

Picture Glossary

cemetery
A place where people are buried after they die.

poppy
A red flower worn to remember soldiers who fought and died for our country.

memorial
Something meant to help remember a person or event.

wreath
Something woven into a circular shape, often displayed as a sign of remembrance.

Index

To Learn More

Learning more is as easy as 1, 2, 3.

1) Go to www.factsurfer.com

2) Enter "MemorialDay" into the search box.

3) Click the "Surf" button to see a list of websites.

With factsurfer.com, finding more information is just a click away.

DISCARD